BLOOMING VERSES
Poetry & Flowers
For Every Month

Written By Creag McMillan
& Illustrated By Heidi Sturgess

BLOOMING LIST

January - Snowdrops - 'Heralds Of Hope'   2

February - Primrose - 'Melting Moments'   10

March - Daffodils - 'Bright Yellow Bells'   18

April - Daisy - 'Whispers of Innocence'   26

May - Hawthorn - 'Guardians of Hearts'   34

June - Honeysuckle - 'Sweet Embrace'   42

July - Larkspur - 'Larkspur's Summer Song'   50

August - Gladiolus - 'Gladiolus In August'   58

September - Aster - 'September's Embrace'   66

October - Marigold - 'Autumn's Warm Embrace'   74

November - Chrysanthemum - 'Flaming Frost'   82

December - Holly - 'Holly's Winter Watch'   90

"To read a poem in January is as lovely as to go for a walk in June."

Jean Paul Satre

January

Heralds of Hope

In winter's grip, a whisper stirs the air,
Snowdrops awaken, fragile and fair.
Through frozen earth, they softly rise,
Delicate yet strong beneath cold skies,
With heads bowed low, then lifting high,
Nature's brave sentinels, winter's ally.

Forerunners of hope when darkness reigns,
Their steadfast blooms, life's sweet refrains.
Whispers of spring beneath crystal snow,
A living tapestry where dreams regrow.

Each bloom, a beacon in winter's hold,
Igniting wonder, a story untold.
Rare bulbs treasured, earth's quiet gift,
Symbols of renewal, spirits to lift.

Tender yet fierce, they lead the way,
Heralds of spring, chasing gloom away.
Through darkest times, their message clear
Hope blossoms anew with each passing year.

The crisp air softens, a subtle change,
As these pioneers of spring arrange
Their silent dance, a wordless song,
Whispering courage to carry on.

So when you spy these drops of snow,
Let your heart with gladness grow.
For in their bloom, so pure and bright,
Lies the promise of returning light.

SNOWDROP
(Galanthus or Milk Flower)
For hope & consolation

These brave little flowers are winter's cheerleaders, popping up through frosty ground when most plants are still hitting the snooze button! Picture tiny white bells dangling from delicate green stems, bobbing in the winter breeze like nature's own fairy lights. Their pure white petals seem to drift like gentle snowflakes, bringing a hint of magic to the coldest months.

These plucky little garden heroes don't wait for spring to make their entrance. They're the first to crash winter's party, sometimes even pushing right through the snow to say "hullo." Here in Yorkshire, snowdrops bring a quiet charm to the garden, appearing each winter by the trees, a reminder that spring is on its way.

Planting Tips

We find that the best way to plant snowdrops is "in the green", just after they've flowered and while their leaves are still vibrant. This method gives them the best chance to establish in your garden. Plant bulbs in early autumn if possible, as this helps them settle in before winter sets in.

Snowdrops thrive in moist, well-drained soil and prefer a partially shaded spot. Plant them under deciduous trees or along pathways where they can spread out and form natural carpets of white each winter.

Snowdrops are resilient and low-maintenance. Once they're happy in their spot, they'll return each year with little need for attention. Simply give them space to spread, and they'll reward you with a dependable winter display. For a bit of help, you can add some compost in early autumn to enrich the soil, but otherwise, they're content to grow on their own.

Snowdrops are among the first flowers to bloom in Europe, earning them the nickname Winter's Herald. Their antifreeze-like properties make them hardy and allow them to survive extreme cold.

In some cultures, snowdrops were seen as bad omens if brought into the home, while others viewed them as protectors against evil spirits.

In Victorian flower language (floriography), snowdrops conveyed sympathy and they were often included in bouquets for grieving friends.

Snowdrops contain galantamine, a compound traditionally used in herbal medicine and now employed in the treatment of Alzheimer's disease.

Other January Flowers

Hellebores

Helleborus

Meet the winter warrior, the Hellebore! Often called the Christmas Rose, these daring blooms push through frost and snow, standing tall with faces tilted skyward. In hues from pure white to deep purple, they scream, "Winter? Bring it on!"

Winter Jasmine

Jasminum Nudiflorum

Winter Jasmine is the garden's own light show, with bright yellow stars cascading down bare branches. These cheerful climbers bloom when others are hibernating, proving that a little sunshine can melt even the frostiest hearts.

Pansies

Viola Tricolor Var Hortensis

These brave little pansies splash winter gardens with vibrant purples, yellows, and whites. Like tiny butterflies, they rest on winter soil, determined to keep the garden buzzing with colour and life.

"February brings the rain,
Thaws the frozen lake again."

Sara Coleridge

February

Melting Moments

In February's tender grasp, they rise,
Primroses peek through brightening skies.
With butter-gold and blush-pink crowns aglow,
Breaking through patches of melting snow.

Sweet fragrance whispers, faint yet clear,
As winter's fortress starts to disappear.
Pale yellow stars pierce the crusty white,
Nature's lanterns in the warming light.

Among the thawing earth, dark and rich,
Where droplets nestle in each hidden niche,
Their petals unfurl, soft as whispered dreams,
Adorning the garden in sunlit gleams.

In dawn's first light, dew-kissed and bold,
Their ruffled faces rimmed with gold
Pierce through the frost with gentle might,
While winter's shadows take their flight.

The morning mist unveils their dance,
As sunbeams give a fleeting glance,
Each bloom a promise, a hope reborn,
Where dormant life awakens with the dawn.

With every primrose bright and new,
Life stirs beneath the morning dew.
In February's warming embrace,
Spring claims her rightful time and place.

PRIMROSE
(Primula Vulgaris)
For new beginnings

Move over winter, the colour parade has arrived! Primroses are like nature's paint palette, splashing the garden with bright yellows, blush pinks, royal purples, and pristine whites. These cheerful little flowers cluster together in happy bunches, with crinkly green leaves fanning out beneath them. Think of primroses as spring's confetti, scattering across borders and woodland floors.

Each flower is a soft edged star with five delicate petals, as if sketched by a child's careful hand. And they aren't shy about sharing their fragrance either, sending gentle hints of spring through the crisp, refreshing air. These garden darlings love to socialise, preferring cosy groups under trees or along pathways.

Give them a sheltered spot with dappled shade, and they'll reward you with a technicolour display sure to lift the spirits. While snowdrops might be winter's brave scouts, primroses are spring's cheerful ambassadors, arriving with their rainbow of colours to signal nature's grand seasonal makeover.

Planting Tips

To get the best from your primroses, plant them in early autumn or spring. They love moist, well-drained soil that's rich in organic matter. Primroses thrive in dappled shade - ideal spots include under deciduous trees, along shaded pathways, or in cool garden borders.

Primroses are low-maintenance but appreciate a little attention. Water regularly during dry spells, especially in warmer months. Adding a layer of mulch in spring can help retain moisture and suppress weeds. Deadheading spent blooms will encourage more flowers, helping these spring ambassadors keep the garden lively. With minimal fuss, they'll brighten your garden for many seasons to come.

The primrose represents youth, new beginnings, and modesty in Victorian flower language.

Associated with the phrase, "I can't live without you," primroses often symbolise first love or deep affection.

In folklore, primroses were thought to be a gateway to the fairy realm, protecting gardens from malevolent spirits.

Other February Flowers

Violet

Viola

The Violet, shy yet stunning, carpets the late winter ground with its delicate charm. With heart-shaped leaves and a fragrance that whispers nostalgia, these tiny blooms bring poetry to February's gardens.

Winter Aconite

Eranthis Hyemalis

Bold and golden, the Winter Aconite is a beacon of sunshine in February's chill. Its cheerful blooms, surrounded by ruffled green collars, bravely push through snow to light up the season.

Magnolia

Grandiflora Magnoliaceae

Elegant goblets of pink and white unfold on bare branches, their petals smooth as silk against spring skies. These massive blooms appear before leaves, filling the air with subtle sweetness while creating living sculptures in awakening gardens.

Crocus

Crocus Sativus

A burst of colour amid frost-kissed earth, the Crocus rises like a phoenix in purples, yellows, and whites. These gems of the garden mark winter's retreat, painting lawns and borders with hope.

"It was one of those March days when the sun shines hot and the wind blows cold: when it is summer in the light, winter in the shade."

Charles Dickens

March

Bright Yellow Bells

Daffodils: Bright Yellow Bells
In fields of green, a radiant chime,
Bright yellow bells proclaim spring's time.
Daffodils sway in the warm sunlight,
Gentle notes of hope, pure and bright.
With petals unfurling in soft embrace,
They dance with the breeze, a joyful grace.

These sunny chimes in nature's choir,
Shatter winter's grip with warming fire.
Their cheerful peal, a vibrant sound,
Awakens life from frozen ground's embrace.
Each bloom a promise, a hopeful spark,
Illuminating the world from winter's dark.

With each bell's nod, the days grow long,
Light returns, a sweet, uplifting song.
In gardens lush and meadows wide,
Their clarion call cannot be denied.
Golden trumpets herald skies of blue,
A symphony of spring, morning-fresh and new.

From whispered tales of love's sweet ways,
They burst to life in spring's bright days.
Their golden hues, so bold and bright,
Nature's passion, a stunning sight.
As sunlight spills across the gentle glade,
Daffodils bloom, no beauty can fade.

From bulbs deep-nestled, year upon year,
These silent bells rise, bringing cheer.
In every bloom, we hear the sound,
Spring's timeless message, profound.
Through storms and frost, their spirit thrives,
A testament to how nature survives.

In fields of green, let our hearts take flight,
As nature sings of spring's pure light.
With every golden bell that sways,
They remind us of brighter days.
In fields of green, let our spirits swell,
As each bright daffodil rings spring's farewell.

DAFFODIL
(Narcissus)
For hope & resilience

Ladies and gentlemen, put your hands together for spring's star performers, the dazzling daffodils. These sunny showstoppers burst onto the garden stage with golden trumpets held high, as if they're ready to take centre stage, showing off their brilliance for all to see. No wallflowers here, each bloom stands proudly atop its sturdy green stem, like a performer in the spotlight.

Think of them as nature's own brass band, with trumpet-shaped centres surrounded by perfectly poised petals that sway in every spring breeze. While many flaunt sunshine-yellow outfits, others dress up in elegant white, bold orange, or even two-tone ensembles. Talk about a fashion statement.

These cheerful performers love putting on a show in groups - the more, the merrier. Plant them in a sunny spot, and they'll return year after year with an even bigger chorus line, transforming you garden into spring's most spectacular concert venue.

After winter's quiet snowdrops and primroses' gentle colour parade, daffodils arrive like nature's own fanfare - bold, bright, and absolutely impossible to ignore. Now, that's what you call making an entrance!

Planting Tips

To get the best from your daffodils, plant them in the autumn, around 4-6 inches deep, with the pointed end facing upwards. Choose a sunny spot with well-drained soil, and daffodils will reward you with a dazzling display year after year. They're very adaptable but thrive in soil rich in organic matter.

Daffodils are low-maintenance, but they appreciate a little attention. Water them regularly in dry periods, especially in their first year. Once they're established, they'll take care of themselves, returning bigger and better each spring. After blooming, allow the foliage to die back naturally as this helps nourish the bulbs for next season's show. Deadheading spent blooms will help them stay tidy, but be patient, as the leaves need to stay to feed the bulb.

Daffodils were originally brought to Britain by the Romans.

The national flower of Wales, daffodils are celebrated on St. David's Day.

A bunch of daffodils symbolises joy and prosperity, friendship and new beginnings.

Other March Flowers

Forsythia
Forsythia Intermedia

A fountain of golden bells cascading down arching branches, Forsythia ignites March gardens with its brilliant display. Before its leaves emerge, these woody stems burst with yellow blooms, creating a luminous curtain of colour that signals spring's triumphant arrival.

Grape Hyacinth
Muscari

Clusters of tiny blue bells rise like miniature grape bunches above slim green leaves. These delicate yet sturdy blooms carpet garden floors with pools of deepest azure. Their sweet, subtle fragrance attracts early pollinators, while their concentrated colour brings intensity to spring's palette.

Tulip
Tulipa

Like painted cups held aloft on strong green stems, tulips herald spring with their bold presence. Available in nearly every colour and pattern imaginable, these elegant blooms transform March gardens into living paintings. Their silken petals unfold to reveal hidden patterns and depths within.

"April, the angel of the months, the young love of the year."

Vita Sackville-West

April

Whispers of Innocence

In meadows bright, where sunlight spills,
Daisies bloom with joy, their laughter thrills.
Their petals dance, a playful serenade,
Nature's soft whispers in the warmest shade.
Each flower a spark in the emerald sea,
A symbol of innocence, wild and free.

Each bloom a smile, pure and sweet,
In nature's embrace, where hearts can meet.
Crowning the fields in white and gold,
Whispering love, tender yet bold.
With every glance, sparkling delight,
A gentle reminder of beauty inside.

Beneath the wide skies, they sway and play,
A symphony of joy in a carefree ballet.
With every petal, secrets unfold,
Reminders of light, and stories retold.
They beckon us closer, inviting the day,
Whispers of innocence, come out and play.

In gardens lush, where sweet dreams take flight,
Colours blend gently in soft morning light.
Their simple beauty, a balm for the soul,
Inviting us to feel, to be truly whole.
Each daisy a story, a moment to share,
A tapestry woven with love and care.

These blossoms fair in morning light,
While new life stirs in spring's delight.
In their presence, we rediscover play,
Welcoming joy with each brightening day.
Through laughter and tears, they stand by our side,
A testament to love that never hides.

Here's to daisies, with their gentle grace,
Each bloom a reflection of youth's embrace.
For in their beauty, innocence stays,
Soft whispers of love, guiding our ways.
In every meadow where they gently sway,
Daisies remind us to cherish today.

Daisies were often exchanged to signify trust.

Daisies were known as "day's eyes"
because they open with the morning sun
and close at Night.

In Norse mythology, daisies are sacred to Freya,
the goddess of love, beauty, and fertility.

DAISY
(Bellis Perennis)
For love, joy & innocence

Meet the friendliest faces in the garden - the delightful daisies! These charming little flowers are nature's answer to a sunny-side-up breakfast, with their pristine white petals radiating out from golden centres like tiny suns scattered across the lawn. And speaking of the sun, these clever blooms are true sun-worshippers, turning their faces to follow the day's light from dawn till dusk.

Don't let their simple looks fool you, daisies are the garden's party planners, popping up in lawns and meadows like cheerful guests who've brought all their friends along. They spread their happiness everywhere, creating magical white carpets that dance in the breeze. No wonder children can't resist picking them for daisy chains and wishes.

These cheerful characters got their name from being the 'day's eye'- opening their petals with the morning sun and closing them snugly at night, as if they're giving the garden a daily wink. Some might call them lawn invaders, but really, they're just enthusiastic huggers of any patch of green they can find!

After the grand theatrical performance of the daffodils, these humble stars remind us that sometimes the sweetest spring moments come in the simplest packages, a lesson in joy delivered by nature's very own sweet smile.

Planting Tips

Daisies thrive in well-drained soil and plenty of sunlight, so plant them in an area with good exposure to the sun. They're quite adaptable, growing happily in lawns or borders. Plant them in spring or early autumn, making sure to space them out so they have room to spread. Daisies are low-maintenance and will multiply over time, creating delightful patches of white wherever they are planted.

Daisies are hardy and require minimal care. Water them during dry spells, but avoid over watering as they prefer well drained soil. After blooming, you can cut back the dead flowers to keep them tidy. They're great at self-seeding, so you'll likely find new plants popping up around your garden each year. If they become too invasive, simply dig them up and divide the clumps to keep them in check.

Other April Flowers

Iris

Iris Sibria

Standing tall like royal sentinels, irises bring architectural elegance to April gardens. Their complex blooms, with falls and standards in contrasting hues, recall the finest silk paintings. Named after the rainbow goddess, they truly capture spring's entire colour palette.

Bluebell

Hyacinthoides

Carpeting woodland floors with waves of nodding blue flowers, bluebells create nature's most enchanting display. Their delicate stems carry clusters of pendant blooms, filling the air with subtle perfume. In dappled sunlight, they create a misty sea of blue beneath awakening trees.

Sweet Pea

Lathyrus Oderatus

Sweet peas are the garden's flirty besties, always smelling like a sweet escape. They twist and twirl up any support they can find, leaving a trail of perfume wherever they go. These social butterflies know how to work a garden party!

Forget-me-not:

Myosotis

Clouds of tiny blue stars hover above low-growing foliage, creating rivers of sky-blue in spring gardens. These charming flowers, with their sunny yellow centres, spread joy throughout borders and paths. Their simple beauty and romantic name have captured hearts for generations.

"Rough winds do shake the darling buds of May, and summer's lease hath all too short a date."

Shakespeare

May

Guardians of Hearts

Upon the May breeze, Hawthorn unfurls,
A sentinel blooming in white-clad swirls.
Its petals soft, a tender disguise,
Yet beneath the blooms, resilience lies.
With fragrance that whispers of stories untold,
A guardian of hearts, both gentle and bold.

In its boughs, the heart finds rest,
Healing each rhythm, each pulse caressed.
A guardian of life, both sharp and sweet,
Each thorn a protector, steadfast and complete.
Through trials and storms, it stands resolute,
A symbol of courage, its roots deeply shoot.

Its roots dig deep in soil and lore,
A symbol of strength that endures evermore.
When May awakens with blossoms in view,
Hawthorn shields the ancient and the true.
In meadows lush, where its branches extend,
It offers solace, a true-hearted friend.

In Celtic wisdom, a sacred sight,
Fairy thorns gleam in pale moonlight.
Its essence a balm, soothing and sure,
A healer's gift, potent and pure.
With each tender bloom, magic unfolds,
A tapestry woven with legends of old.

Not a fragile bloom, but nature's knight,
Defending the soul through day and night.
Through ages long, its virtues endure—
Hawthorn: steadfast, strong, and sure.
As spring breathes life into the waking land,
It paves the way for blooms that brightly stand.

So let us honour this guardian strong,
Whose ancient wisdom guides us along.
In the dance of the seasons, let hearts take flight,
Embracing the magic of day and night.
For in Hawthorn's embrace, we find our place,
As spring's grand pageant unfolds with grace,
Welcoming summer's warmth, a gentle trace.

HAWTHORN
(Crataegus)
For love, protection & fertility

Step aside, spring flowers, here comes the wise elder of the hedgerow. Hawthorn arrives like nature's own wedding celebration, draping itself in clouds of white or pink blossoms that turn every country lane into a magical bridal aisle. Each delicate flower cluster is a miniature bouquet, sending out sweet perfume invitations to every bee and butterfly in the neighbourhood.

But this isn't just another pretty face in the garden - Hawthorn is the keeper of ancient tales and mysteries. While the daisies play in meadows below, this enchanting tree stands tall and proud, weaving its thorny branches into a protective embrace around spring's secret gardens. Later, it'll dress itself in rubies, those bright red haws that gleam like treasure in autumn's light.

Think of Hawthorn as May's master of ceremonies, arriving just in time to crown spring's festivities with its spectacular flowering finale. It's the perfect blend of wild grace and gentle charm, equally at home in a royal garden or a windswept hillside. After the cheerful dance of daffodils and the sweet simplicity of daisies, Hawthorn steps forward as spring's grand finale - part guardian, part enchanter, and absolutely dressed to impress!

Planting Tips

Hawthorn thrives in well-drained soil and can tolerate a variety of conditions, from full sun to partial shade. While it's not particularly fussy about the soil, it does best in slightly acidic to neutral soil. Plant Hawthorn in early autumn or spring, making sure to give it plenty of space to grow. It's a slow-growing tree, but once established, it will thrive for many years.

Hawthorn is relatively low-maintenance once established. Water it during dry spells, but avoid over watering, as it doesn't like being too soggy. Prune Hawthorn in late winter or early spring to maintain its shape, but avoid cutting back too much, as its thorny branches can be difficult to handle. In the autumn, enjoy the bright red haws as they appear, which are often used in herbal remedies or simply enjoyed as a beautiful feature of the tree.

A symbol of hope, protection and happiness, hawthorn branches were often woven into garlands for May Day celebrations.

Also known as the May Tree, it has strong ties to fertility and renewal in Celtic traditions.

In folklore, hawthorn was believed to guard against evil spirits, making it a popular choice for protective hedges.

Other May Flowers

Lilac
Syringa Vulgaris

Cascading clusters of tiny star-shaped blooms create a fragrant waterfall of colour in spring gardens. Their sweet intoxicating perfume, more complex and romantic than Lavender's herbal notes, drifts on warm breezes to herald the arrival of May. From pristine white to deepest purple, higlighted by the classic lilac hue, these generous shrubs unfold pointed panicles of hundreds of tiny flowers and soft heart shaped leaves, creating natural bouquets.

Peony
Paeonia

Like gathered silk, peony blooms unfold layer upon layer of petals to create flowers of extraordinary richness. Their heavy heads, in shades from pure white to deepest crimson, fill May gardens with sumptuous beauty and subtle fragrance. Each bloom is a celebration of spring's abundance.

Columbine

Aquilegia

Dancing on delicate stems, these intricate blooms seem almost otherworldly. Their spurred petals create elaborate stars in shades from deepest purple to palest pink. These graceful flowers attract early butterflies while adding an air of enchantment to spring gardens.

Lily of the Valley

Convallaria Majalis

Dainty white bells hang beneath broad green leaves, filling May gardens with their incomparable fragrance. These woodland treasures spread quietly through shaded spots, creating colonies of pristine blooms.

"And what is so rare as a day in June? Then if ever, come perfect days."

Emily Dickinson

June

Sweet Embrace

In June's warm glow, where blossoms entwine,
Honeysuckle blooms, a nectar divine.
With tendrils that climb and sweet fragrance spread,
They weave through the garden, where memories tread.
A symbol of love in the soft summer air,
Inviting all hearts to linger and share.

As twilight descends, their perfume awakes,
Whispers of warmth in the stillness it makes.
Golden and cream, in the sun's gentle light,
They dance with the breeze, a soft, sweet delight.
In tangled embrace, they cradle the night,
Filling our souls with gentle respite.

Amongst the green leaves, their blossoms unfold,
Stories of summers and secrets retold.
With each tender petal, a promise is made,
Of sweet moments cherished, of joys that won't fade.
They beckon us closer, with laughter and song,
In the heart of the garden, where we all belong.

Their vibrant hues paint the twilight sky,
As fireflies flicker and soft breezes sigh.
A tapestry woven with warmth and with grace,
Honeysuckle's charm, a warm, sweet embrace.
In the hush of the evening, they softly bloom,
Filling the night air with their sweet perfume.

So let us gather these blossoms each day,
With open hearts, let our spirits play.
In their presence, we find joy anew,
As honeysuckle whispers, "I'm here for you."
A reminder of love in the summer's embrace,
As we weave through the seasons, a dance we all trace.

As summer unfolds, let us not forget,
The sweetness of honeysuckle, never a threat.
For in their soft petals and fragrant delight,
Lies the promise of love, shining bright.
In the cycle of life, where blossoms entwine,
Honeysuckle sings of a love that is thine.

HONEYSUCKLE
(Lonicera Periclymenum)
For love, affection & happiness

Sliding into summer comes our sweetest charmer – the heavenly honeysuckle! This romantic soul dances its way up walls and twirls around trellises, sending out waves of perfume that make evening gardens feel like nature's very own perfumery. Each flower is a delicate trumpet of gold, white, or pink, as if summer decided to hang tiny jewels in the air, just for our delight.

These fragrant acrobats aren't content with staying grounded – they climb and weave their way skyward, creating secret bowers where butterflies dance and hummingbirds hover like tiny love notes on wings. Talk about a summer romance! Their sweet nectar is summer's own dessert menu, served in dainty tubes that only the most nimble garden visitors can reach.

By day, they're sun-kissed climbers reaching for the sky, but as dusk falls, they really come into their own. That's when they release their sweetest perfume, turning every garden corner into an enchanted evening paradise. Who needs fairy lights when you've got honeysuckle's lanterns glowing in the twilight?

After May's majestic displays, these gentle performers remind us that summer's magic isn't just about grand gestures – sometimes it's found in the gentle twist of a vine and the sweet whisper of perfume on a warm evening breeze.

Planting Tips

Honeysuckle thrives in well-drained soil and enjoys full sun to partial shade. It's a versatile climber and can grow in a variety of garden settings, from trellises and fences to walls and arbors. Plant it in early spring or autumn, allowing enough space for its vines to spread and weave.

Honeysuckle is relatively low-maintenance but benefits from regular pruning to keep its shape and encourage new growth. Prune it after flowering to maintain its size and to prevent it from becoming too unruly. Water it during dry spells, but avoid overwatering, as it prefers slightly drier soil. In winter, cut back any dead or damaged growth to ensure a healthy and vibrant bloom come spring.

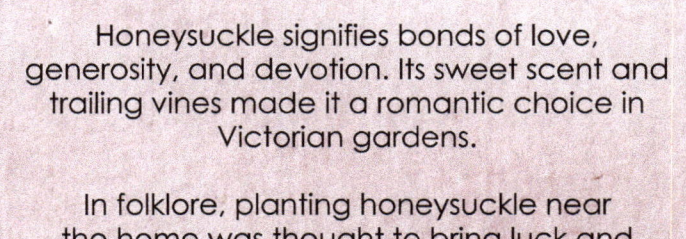

Honeysuckle signifies bonds of love, generosity, and devotion. Its sweet scent and trailing vines made it a romantic choice in Victorian gardens.

In folklore, planting honeysuckle near the home was thought to bring luck and ward off negative energy.

Other June Flowers

Rose
Rosa

The very essence of summer captured in layers of perfumed petals. From simple wild forms to elaborate hybrid blooms, roses bring both sophistication and romance to June gardens. Their rich fragrance and varied colours have earned them their title as queens of the garden.

Hydrangea
Hortensia

Big, bold, brash — the hydrangea is the Hydra of Drama. It lives large in its fluffy clouds of pink, blue, or white, making every garden its stage. Gratitude? Apologies? Maybe. But really, it's just here to werk it!

Mountain Cornflower
Centaurea Montana

Delicate blue flowers float like butterflies above silver-green foliage. Their ragged petals catch the light, creating pools of sky blue in summer borders. These hardy plants bring a touch of alpine meadows to any garden setting.

Foxglove
Digitalis Purpurea

Towers of spotted bells rise through June borders, each throat speckled with intricate patterns. These stately flowers bring vertical drama and woodland charm to early summer gardens. Bees disappear into their tubular blooms, emerging dusted with pollen.

"The summer looks out from her brazen tower.
Through flashing bars of July."

Francis Thompson

July

Larkspur's Summer Song

In summer's warmth, where colours ignite,
Larkspur stands tall, a knightly sight.
With spurs of blue and violet hues,
Each bloom adorned by morning's dews.
A tapestry woven where sunlight plays,
Nature's own story of fleeting days.

Through fields and gardens, proudly they stand,
Like noble sentries across the land.
Each delicate petal, a soft embrace,
Stirs memories that cascade through this place.
Through borders wild, they cheerfully bloom,
Chasing shadows away, defying the gloom.

Sturdy stems reaching toward the sky,
Symbols of openness, never shy.
Though brief their reign, they make hearts skip,
As summer secrets softly slip.
In bright clusters, joy intertwines,
While bees hum sweetly their summer rhymes.

Sweet fragrance drifts on warm July eves,
Where winding paths weave through the leaves.
Among the roses, proud and tall,
They answer summer's ancient call.
From dusk until dawn, through golden light,
Their colours paint the heart's delight.

When you spy these blooms so true,
Remember summer mornings, new,
When every garden held its spell,
And every flower had tales to tell.
Those golden days stretched endless then,
When wonder lived in children's ken.

As seasons turn with each passing year,
Larkspur returns, its message clear:
Of garden dreams and open hearts,
Of beauty blooming as time departs.
In delicate strength and skies of blue,
Larkspur's sweet song forever rings true.

LARKSPUR
(Delphinium)
For happiness, fun & humour

Move aside, garden wallflowers - the tall, dark and handsome Larkspur has arrived! These magnificent bloomers are summer's answer to a firework display, sending up spectacular spikes of colour that shoot straight for the sky. Think of them as nature's skyscrapers, dressed in their finest blues, purples, pinks and whites, standing as proud as palace guards but with much better outfits!

These fashionable giants aren't content with simply growing in the garden - they're reaching for the stars, darling! While other flowers spread outwards, Larkspurs go up, up, and up some more, creating their own flowery high-rise apartments where bees can practise their vertical parking. With their deeply cut leaves and soaring flower spikes, they're like the aristocrats of the summer garden - impossibly elegant, rather dramatic, and definitely not afraid to stand out in a crowd. Some of these show-offs can grow taller than your average eight-year-old, which is quite the party trick for a flower!

After honeysuckle's sweet summer romance, these bold beauties remind us that sometimes love reaches for the heights - straight up towards the summer sky with all the confidence of a flower that knows exactly how fabulous it is.

Planting Tips

Larkspurs thrive in sunny locations, ideally receiving at least 6 hours of sunlight a day. Plant them in well-draining soil that's slightly alkaline or neutral. If you have heavy clay soil, mix in some compost to improve drainage. Sow seeds directly into the soil in early spring, planting them about 1/4 inch deep. Space seeds 6 inches apart to give them room to grow tall and proud.

Larkspurs need regular watering, especially in dry weather, but be sure not to over water them. Fertilize with a balanced, slow-release fertilizer in spring to kickstart their growth. A mid-season feed can help them maintain their strength and height.

Remove spent flowers to keep your Larkspur looking tidy and encourage more blooms. If you want them to self-seed
for the following year, leave some flowers to naturally go to seed by late summer. Larkspurs are annuals in most climates but can be treated as perennials in milder regions.

Larkspur symbolises an open heart, positivity, and strong bonds of love.

Its vibrant colours were associated with levity and light-heartedness in Victorian times.

The name larkspur comes from the flower's resemblance to a lark's claw.

Other July Flowers

Sunflower
Helianthus Annus

Like miniature suns floating on tall stems, these magnificent blooms track the day's light. Their massive flower heads, surrounded by golden petals, provide food for birds and beauty for gardeners. They embody summer's warmth and nature's generosity.

Geranium
Pelagonium

Clusters of jewel-toned flowers dance above deeply cut foliage, creating waves of colour through summer gardens. These hardy perennials offer endless varieties, from tiny alpine forms to spreading border plants. Their reliable blooms add both structure and movement to July's display.

Lavender

Lavender Augustifolia

The sleepy dream of the serene garden, Lavender murmurs calm into winter's stillness. Its soft, silvery leaves cradle a whisper of spring, while its gentle fragrance lulls the world into peaceful reflection

Calla Lily

Zantedeschia

Spiral blooms rise from arrow-shaped leaves, bringing exotic grace to summer borders. Their sculptural form and subtle colours provide sophisticated beauty for many months. These architectural plants offer drama in both flower and foliage.

Water Lily

Nymphaea

Floating serenely on still water, these exotic blooms open each morning to reveal jewel-like centres. Their large pads create stepping stones for dragonflies, while their flowers range from pristine white to deep crimson. They bring a sense of tranquility to high summer gardens.

"Today is the first of August. It is hot, steamy and wet. It is raining. I am tempted to write a poem."

Sylvia Plath

August

Gladiolus In August

Gladiolus blooms in summer's light,
Tall and proud, colours ignite.
With petals poised, a whisper of hope,
They rise above, resilient, they cope.
In August's warmth, they stand so bold,
A tale of strength in petals told.

As days grow long and sunlight gleams,
We gather moments, chase our dreams.
With laughter soft, adrift in air,
Each fleeting second, a joy laid bare.
In playful breezes, friendships bound,
In gladiolus, our hearts are found.

When storms roll in with thunder's roar,
We anchor deep and grow once more.
Through trials faced, we learn to stand,
Embracing life, hand in hand.
With every struggle, colours blend,
In summer's dance, we find our friends.

As twilight hues paint skies aglow,
We watch the summer, gentle, slow.
In gardens bright with vibrant grace,
We treasure each familiar place.
Through every petal, love's embrace,
In August's heart, we find our space.

In whispers soft, memories flow,
Of laughter shared, of seeds we sow.
Each gladiolus, a story spun,
A testament to battles won.
As days grow short, we hold them tight,
In every bloom, there shines a light.

Through summer's song and August's cheer,
We find the strength to persevere.
In gladiolus blooms so bright,
We see the beauty of our fight.
With petals raised toward the sun,
We celebrate what we've become.

GLADIOLUS
(Gladiolus or Little Sword)
For strength, victory & pride

Ave Caesar! The gladioli have entered the garden arena. These magnificent blooms, true gladiators of the flower world (and yes, that's exactly where they got their name), march into late summer like a parade of colourful warriors. Their flowers line up like precious jewels on tall stems, unfurling their blooms from bottom to top as if they're putting on nature's most elegant slow-motion show. Dressed in everything from fierce reds to delicate pinks, regal purples to sunshine yellows, each spike is like a tower of butterfly wings caught in mid-flutter. Some even sport fancy patterns, as if they've decorated themselves for battle in summer's grandest tournament.

These natural sword-dancers carry themselves with all the grace and power of their namesake warriors, but their only conquest is winning the hearts of every garden visitor. Give them a sunny stage, and they'll reward you with a performance that makes even the butterflies stop and stare. After Larkspur's skyward reach, these elegant warriors show us that summer still has plenty of drama up its sleeve - bringing a touch of Roman theatre to the English garden just when we thought the season couldn't get any more Spectacular.

Planting Tips

Gladiolus prefer sunny spots where they can bask in the full glory of the sun. Plant corms about 3 to 4 inches deep in well-drained soil, spaced 4 to 6 inches apart. Choose a location with good air circulation to prevent fungal diseases. Plant them in early spring, after the last frost has passed.

Water Gladiolus regularly, but sparingly. They like consistent moisture but should never sit in waterlogged soil. Water at the base to avoid getting the foliage too wet. You can add compost to the soil before planting to give them a good start, then feed your gladioli with a balanced fertilizer during their growing season to encourage strong stems and plenty of blooms.

As Gladiolus grow, they may need stakes or plant supports to help keep the tall stems upright, especially during windy weather. Remove spent flowers to encourage fresh blooms. Leave the flowers to go to seed by late summer, or dig up the corms after the first frost and store them in a dry, cool place until next Spring.

A symbol of strength, honour, and remembrance, gladiolus embodies integrity and resilience.

Often called the sword lily, it was popular in Roman times for its bold, upright form.

Gladiolus flowers were thought to represent moral integrity and infatuation in equal measure.

Other August Flowers

Poppy

Papaverus

Paper-thin petals in brilliant hues dance on slender stems, each flower lasting just days but leaving distinctive seedheads. Their fleeting beauty and vivid colours capture the essence of late summer abundance. From familiar red to exotic purple, they bring drama to August gardens.

Montbretia

Crocosmia

Sprays of fiery orange flowers dance on arching stems, adding late summer warmth to borders. Their sword-like leaves provide structure, while their star-shaped blooms catch August's golden light. These vibrant flowers bridge the gap between summer and autumn.

Cosmos

Cosmos Bipinnatus

Dancing on tall stems, these daisy-like flowers in white and pink continue blooming until hard frost. Their feathery foliage adds texture to borders, while their simple flowers charm with unaffected grace. They embody October's lingering warmth and beauty.

Dahlia

Dahlia Pinnata

Perfectly formed blooms in an endless array of colours and forms dominate late summer borders. From simple single flowers to complex cactus varieties, dahlias provide continuous colour until first frost. Their geometric perfection and rich hues epitomize August's mature beauty.

"September: it was the most beautiful of words, he'd always felt, evoking orange flowers, swallows, and regret."

Alexander Theroux

September

September's Embrace

Aster blooms as summer wanes,
With twilight hues where sunlight drains.
In gardens kissed by autumn's breath,
They whisper tales of life and death.
A symbol of change, time's gentle trace,
In September's cool, they find their place.

The days grow short, the shadows long,
As autumn weaves its quiet song.
With every breeze, the leaves will dance,
In crisp, fresh air, we take our chance.
We gather close, in warmth we find,
The beauty of hearts, forever kind.

With every bloom, memories swell,
Of summer's warmth, we bid farewell.
In laughter shared and stories spun,
We trace the strength of all we've done.
In vibrant hues, our spirits rise,
As asters bloom beneath soft skies.

The harvest moon begins to glow,
And nature's palette starts to show.
In fields of purple, blue, and white,
We celebrate the autumn night.
With every petal, love's refrain,
In autumn's arms, we feel the gain.

As twilight deepens, stars appear,
We hold our loved ones ever near.
In whispered dreams and quiet grace,
We find our place in time and space.
Through every change, our bonds will grow,
In aster's bloom, our love will show.

Aster blooms as autumn calls,
With colours bright as summer falls.
A tribute to the love we share,
In every petal, tender care.
As September wraps us in its charms,
With aster's grace, we find our arms.

ASTERS
(Symphyotrichum, Astrum or Star)
For patience, love & wisdom

The Starry-Eyed Dancers of the Garden. Just when summer's grand performance seems to be taking its final bow, who should twirl onto the stage but the starry eyed Asters! These dainty dancers arrive like nature's own galaxy, scattering themselves across gardens in a constellation of purples, blues, pinks, and whites. Each flower is a perfect little star, as if the night sky couldn't wait until evening to show off its sparkle.

While other flowers may be thinking about their autumn rest, these energetic performers are just getting started. They're the life and soul of the late-summer garden party, hosting farewell feasts for butterflies and bees before winter draws near. Talk about saving the best for last - these blooms turn every border into a stellar celebration.

Named after the Greek word for 'star', they certainly live up to their celestial reputation. Whether they're performing solo in cottage gardens or dancing in meadow choruses, they sparkle and shine like summer's final fireworks display. After our gladioli's grand Roman parade, these heavenly beauties remind us that every garden deserves a star-studded finale - bringing a touch of cosmic magic to those precious golden days when summer whispers its sweet goodbye.

Planting Tips

Asters are best planted in spring, after the last frost, to give them a full season to settle in before their late-summer performance. Choose a sunny spot with well-drained soil, as they thrive in sunlight and need space to spread. Space the plants about 18 to 24 inches apart.

Asters require regular watering during dry spells. They prefer moist soil but dislike standing water. Apply a balanced fertilizer in early spring to encourage strong growth, with a slow-release fertilizer working best. Deadhead spent flowers regularly to prolong blooming and keep the plant tidy. In late autumn, trim the plants back to about 6 inches to prepare them for winter. While Asters are relatively hardy, mulching around the base can help protect the roots from frost.

Representing wisdom, patience, and elegance, asters were a favourite in Victorian bouquets.

Asters are named after the Greek word for star, reflecting their striking, star-shaped blooms. In Greek mythology, asters were born of stardust, connecting them to Celestial themes.

Other September Flowers

Stonecrop
Sedum

Flat heads of tiny stars create plates of colour, attracting late butterflies and bees. Their succulent foliage provides interest throughout the year, while their autumn blooms offer essential late season nectar. These tough plants thrive in the most challenging conditions.

Fuchsia
Fuchsia Coccinea

Dangling like exotic earrings, these intricate flowers combine deep pinks and purples in perfect harmony. Their ballet skirt blooms dance in September breezes, bringing colour to shaded corners. Each flower is a masterpiece of natural Engineering.

Clematis

Ranunculaceae

Late-flowering varieties cover walls and fences with sheets of star shaped blooms. Their climbing habit brings September colour to vertical spaces, while their feathery seed heads extend interest into winter. These versatile plants link summer's abundance with autumn's approaching change.

Morning Glory

Ipomoea

Look at me, look at me! I'm the early bird of the flower world. Morning Glories burst open with the sunrise, showing off their blues, purples, and pinks like they've just rolled out of bed looking effortlessly fabulous. By afternoon, they're all, "That's enough for today," and gracefully close shop. Prima donnas? Absolutely. Completely reserved yet unapologetically themselves, they know exactly when to make their exit.

"October is the treasure of the year, and all the months pay bounty to her store."

Lucy Maud Montgomery

October

Autumn's Warm Embrace

Autumn glowing, saturated light,
Marigolds bursting forth, this joyful sight.
Ruffled petals, sun-kissed hue,
October's treasure, vibrant and true.
Their golden crowns, a warm embrace,
A touch of cheer in every space.

Their scent dances in the crisp, cool air,
Weaving memories beyond compare.
In gardens, their bright faces beam,
Like sunlit fragments of a dream.
Each bloom, a symbol of pure delight,
A flame that flickers through the night.

Through cultures rich, they leave their mark,
A bridge between the light and dark.
With every petal, a story's told,
Of warmth, of love, of hearts made bold.
In every garden, they stand so proud,
As autumn whispers through the crowd.

They rise from earth, where sunlight flows,
With vibrant strength, their beauty grows.
In rich soil, their roots take hold,
A sign of life in days grown cold.
As evenings shorten, they still shine,
Their golden warmth, a gift divine.

Marigolds, bright as evening stars,
Remind us of the paths we've walked so far.
Their colors blaze, their scent remains,
A joy that lingers, breaks the chains.
In their glow, our hearts take flight,
As autumn wraps us in its light.

With every breeze that stirs the leaves,
Marigolds dance, as nature grieves.
In quiet moments, we take our place,
In their golden warmth, we find our grace.
As October wanes, they still stand tall,
A symbol of warmth through it all.

MARIGOLD
(Calendula Officinalis)
For sunlight, power & strength

A burst of autumn cheer. Hold onto your gardening hats - here come autumn's cheerleaders in their magnificent orange and gold uniforms. Marigolds bounce into the garden like little suns that have decided to grow right out of the ground, sporting ruffled pompoms in every warm shade from sunrise yellow to sunset red. These plucky performers don't just bloom - they absolutely dazzle!

Talk about dedication to the show - while other flowers are taking their final curtain calls, these bright sparks keep the garden glowing right until Jack Frost makes his first appearance. They're like tiny torches lighting autumn's path, with their feathery foliage doing a Mexican wave every time the breeze passes by. And don't let their pretty faces fool you - these flowers are garden superheroes in disguise. They patrol vegetable patches like cheerful security guards, their spicy scent sending unwanted pests packing. Who knew such charming flowers could also be such clever defenders?

After the Asters' starry spectacle, these sunny champions remind us that autumn isn't about fading away - it's about putting on the brightest, boldest show of the year. Now that's what we call going out with a bang!

Planting Tips

Marigolds are as easy to plant as they are to love! Plant them in a sunny spot with well-drained soil for maximum blooms. They thrive in almost any soil type but prefer slightly acidic to neutral conditions. If you're planting them from seed, start indoors about six weeks before the last frost date, or sow them directly into the garden after the danger of frost has passed. Space the plants about 12 to 18 inches apart to allow for proper air circulation.

Caring for marigolds is a breeze. They are low-maintenance and drought-tolerant, making them perfect for busy gardeners. Water them regularly, but be careful not to overwater as they dislike soggy roots. Deadhead spent blooms to encourage more flowers throughout the season. Marigolds benefit from occasional feeding with a balanced fertilizer to keep them vibrant and healthy. If you're growing them in containers, ensure they have enough space to grow, and consider repotting if they start to outgrow their pots.

Marigolds symbolise warmth, creativity, and passion but also have ties to grief and remembrance.

In Mexican culture, marigolds are central to Día de los Muertos, guiding spirits back to the living world.

Known as the herb of the sun, marigolds were often used in ancient rituals to honour the divine.

Other October Flowers

Salvia

Salvia Officinalis

Spikes of interested of blue or scarlet flowers persist through autumn's first frosts. Their aromatic foliage and architectural form provide structure to October gardens. These hardy plants offer essential late colour and attract the season's last pollinators.

Petunia

Petunioideae

Trumpet-shaped blooms cascade in waves of purple, pink and white, their faces painted with starry patterns. These persistent flowers spill from containers and borders, releasing their gentle perfume into Autumn's cooling evenings.

Alpine Violet

Cyclamnen

Cyclamen are the cool kids cycling along mountain tops with violet vibes and a rebel streak. They twirl their petals backward like they're too cool for gravity, bringing their mountain swagger to any garden space. Resilient and a little mysterious - that's just how they roll!

Hyacinth

Hyacinth Orientalis

"Pick me, pick me, pick me!" shout the hyacinths, the drama queens of the flower world. They strut into spring with colours for every mood — purple for deep feels, blue for chill, and white for angel vibes. Their scent? Pure showbiz sparkle!

"No shade, no shine, no butterflies, no bees. No fruits, no flowers, no leaves, no birds - November!"

Thomas Hood

November

Flaming Frost

In autumn's glow, chrysanthemums rise,
Bold blooms that gleam 'neath cooling skies.
Their petals blaze, a fiery hue,
Amber, crimson, and rusted too.
A quiet defiance, they softly stay,
Stalwart through autumn's fading day.

Through frost they keep,
Their vigour deep,
A flame in fields whilst others sleep.

November's winds may howl and sigh,
But mums stand firm as green things die.
Each stem holds fast, each blossom sings,
A fleeting joy as the season swings.
A lesson in strength, so fierce, so true,
Each petal whispers, "You'll make it through."

When gardens wane,
And leaves are slain,
They hold their ground through wind and rain.

Rooted deep in November's earth,
Their fiery hues give life its worth.
A bold finale, before the snow,
They bid the garden one last glow.
As nights grow long and days grow dim,
They stand, resilient to the brim.

When shadows fall,
They still stand tall,
Bright torches blazing against it all.

CHRYSANTHEMUMS
(Dendranthema Grandiflorum)
For happiness, long life & joy

Ladies and gentlemen, presenting autumn's prima ballerinas - the captivating chrysanthemum. While other flowers take their final bows, these sophisticated stars are just warming up, unfurling their petals like elaborate tutus in every shade from snow white to deepest burgundy. Some sport perfect pompoms, others twist their petals like exotic spiders, and some spread their rays like starburst fireworks - talk about saving the best choreography for last.

These autumn aristocrats didn't just join the garden party - they ARE the party. Whether they're performing elegant solos in patio pots or staging a full ensemble in flower beds, they transform the cooling days into nature's own fashion show. Each bloom is like a perfectly crafted piece of art, as if autumn decided to show off everything it learned from the seasons before.

And such stamina! While our marigold cheerleaders keep the garden's spirit bright, these elegant performers take centre stage for the season's grand finale, dancing on even as the first frost threatens to draw the curtain. They're autumn's own confirmation that the year's most spectacular show comes just before the interval!

After all the garden's earlier performances, from spring's shy snowdrops to summer's bold gladioli, these magnificent mums remind us that nature always saves a special encore for those who stick around to watch the whole show!

Planting Tips

Plant chrysanthemums in the spring, after the last frost, to give them plenty of time to establish their roots before the autumn show begins. Alternatively, you can plant them in late summer if you're aiming for a fall bloom. Choose a bright sunny location with well-drained soil and water regularly at the base.

Fertilize chrysanthemums in the spring to encourage strong, healthy growth. Once they start to bloom, switch to a high-potassium fertilizer to help promote flowering. Pinch back the stems in early summer to encourage more blooms. Once blooming is complete, cut back the plants to around six inches to prepare them for winter. In colder climates, mulch around the base to protect the roots from freezing.

Representing friendship, loyalty, and longevity, chrysanthemums were favoured in Victorian friendship bouquets.

In Chinese culture, chrysanthemums symbolise nobility and are a key part of autumn festivals.

Chrysanthemums are associated with royalty in Japan and are celebrated during the Festival of Happiness.

Other October Flowers

Camellia

Camellia Japonica

Like roses carved from wax, these winter-blooming shrubs defy the season. Their glossy evergreen leaves provide year-round structure, while their perfect blooms bring colour to November gardens. Each flower opens to reveal layers of petals in shades from pure white to deepest red.

Amaryllis

Hippeastrum

Giant trumpet blooms on thick stems bring tropical splendour to November's shortening days. Their dramatic flowers in rich reds, pure whites, and striped patterns offer indoor colour as gardens fade. Each bulb produces multiple blooms of outstanding size and beauty.

Anemone

Anemone Coronaria

In the UK, anemones can still be found blooming in November, particularly the hardy varieties suited to cooler temperatures. Their delicate petals, often in shades of white, pink, or purple, bring a soft elegance to gardens and natural landscapes. Despite the encroaching winter, these resilient flowers continue to provide a splash of colour, brightening the season before the frost fully sets in.

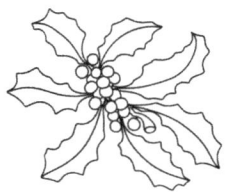

"Of all the months of the year, there is not a month half so welcome to the young, or so full of happy associations, as the last month of the year."

Elizabeth Gaskell

December

Holly's Winter Watch

Deep in December's fading haze,
Holly stands through winter's maze,
Each leaf a steadfast shield, so green,
Sharp-tipped sentries rarely seen,
Guardian of the frozen ground,
Silent watcher, wisdom crowned.

Through bitter frost and biting cold,
Those thorned leaves, so fierce and bold,
Pierce the mist of morning light,
Armoured sentinels, winter-bright,
While crimson berries catch the sun,
Like drops of dawn when day's begun.

Beneath the snow that drifts and swells,
Its branches cradle ancient spells,
As birds find shelter in its shade,
Safe within the barricade,
Of interlaced and sturdy boughs,
Where winter's secrets make their vows.

Each glossy leaf reflects the sky,
As clouds and stars go wheeling by,
While time stands still in frozen air,
And frost weaves patterns, crystal-rare,
Across the darkness of each blade
That nature's patient craft has made.

When shadows lengthen, day by day,
And winter storms sweep in to stay,
The berries shine like signal fires,
Above the snow in scarlet spires,
A feast for thrush and wandering wren,
Until spring wakens once again.

So Holly keeps its patient way,
Through longest night and shortest day,
Each leaf a lesson time has taught
Of strength and grace so dearly bought,
Standing firm where cold winds scream,
Eternal guardian, evergreen.

HOLLY
(Ilex Aquifolium)
For endurance & change

When winter draws its darkest curtain, behold the evergreen guardian of the sleeping garden - the magnificent Holly! While other plants dream beneath their blankets of frost, this proud sentinel stands watchful and radiant, dressed in glossy green armour adorned with rubies. Each spiny leaf catches the winter light like nature's own stained glass, while clusters of berries glow like tiny lanterns in the December gloom.

Don't be fooled by those shy spring flowers playing hide-and-seek among the leaves - Holly is the master of the long game. Those modest blooms are just whispered promises of the winter jewels to come. Patient and wise, it transforms its secret spring blossoms into a feast of scarlet berries, a banquet table set for winter's feathered guests. This ancient keeper of yuletide mysteries does more than stand pretty in wreaths and garlands - it's a sanctuary in the quiet months, offering shelter to drowsy birds and late-season butterflies.

Like a Christmas story come to life, it sparkles with frost and tradition, keeping winter's magic alive in every spiny leaf and bright berry. After autumn's grand finale, Holly steps forward as winter's own royal guard - dressed in ceremonial green and scarlet, standing proud until spring's brave snowdrops herald another year of garden enchantment!

Planting Tips

Holly should be planted in the autumn or early spring, allowing it to establish its roots before the extremes of winter or summer. Choose a spot with well-drained soil that is partial to full sun. While holly can tolerate some shade, it thrives best in sunlight. Ensure the soil is acidic to slightly alkaline for optimal growth. Holly is hardy and can withstand frost, but it's a good idea to mulch around the base to protect the roots from severe cold.

Water holly regularly during the growing season, especially during dry spells. Holly prefers moist but well-drained soil. Feed holly with a balanced fertilizer in early spring to promote healthy growth. Holly typically doesn't require much pruning, but it can be trimmed and shaped in late winter or early spring before new growth starts.

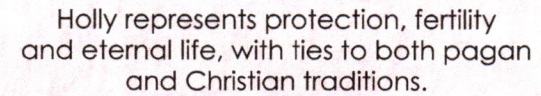

Holly represents protection, fertility and eternal life, with ties to both pagan and Christian traditions.

A central part of Yuletide celebrations, holly was believed to shelter fairies and ward off evil spirits.

In medieval times, holly was used medicinally to treat fevers and Ward off nightmares.

Other December Flowers

Rhododendron

Oleander

Clusters of bright pink and magenta flowers, crown dark evergreen leaves, defying winter's quiet. These noble shrubs create domes of unexpected colour above glossy foliage, bringing warmth to December's muted garden.

Witch Hazel

Hamamelis Hazel

Spidery flowers in yellow or orange appear on naked branches, glowing in winter light. Their subtle fragrance carries surprisingly far in cold air, while their unusual form adds interest to December gardens. These late bloomers prove that nature's beauty persists through all seasons.

Narcissus

Narcissus Pseudonarcissus

Forced bulbs bring spring's promise to midwinter, their fragrant blooms filling rooms with sweetness. These early harbingers of spring offer hope during December's darkness. Their pristine petals and golden cups recall sunnier days to come.

Viburnum

Laurastinus

Clusters of pink-tinged flowers appear on bare winter branches, their sweet fragrance carrying on cold air. These tough shrubs bloom when little else dares, their flowers lasting well into winter. Their presence reminds us that life continues even in December's quiet.

"Art is not what you see, but what you make others see."

Edgar Degas

"Where flowers bloom, so does hope."

Lady Bird Johnson

Evans Webb

Blooming Verses
First published by Evans Webb
© Creag McMillian and Heidi Sturgess 2024

The right of Creag McMillan and Heidi Sturgess as author and illustrator of this book has been asserted by them in accordance with the Copyright, Designs and Patent Act 1988.

All rights reserved. No part of this book may be reproduced, transmitted, or stored in an information retrieval system in any form or by any means, graphic, electronic or mechanical, including photocopying, taping and recording, without prior written permission from the publisher.

ISBN 978-0-9931480-1-9

www.evanswebb.co.uk

www.ingramcontent.com/pod-product-compliance
Lightning Source LLC
Chambersburg PA
CBHW051551010526
44118CB00022B/2664